MEL BAY PRESE[NTS]
LATIN AMERICAN
SONGS FOR GUITAR

By Jerry Silverman

19 countries represented
with all lyrics in Spanish and singable English

CONTENTS

3

El Carretero
The Cartman

The *chacarera* is a country dance that originated in the northern provinces of Argentina, during the latter part of the 19th century. Its rural roots are evident from its name *chacra,* the word for farm.

Argentina - Song and Accompaniment

Chacarera

Ca - rre - te - ro, ca - rre - te - ro, ca - rre
Oh, you cart-man, oh, you cart - man, oh, you
te - ro, ca - rre - te - ro, e - se
cart-man, oh, you cart - man, that rose -

te - ro de jun - cal, el o - to - ño trai - cio-
cart-man, roll - ing free, it's the treach-'rous au - tumn
ro - sal es mi_a - mor. El o - to - ño trai - cio-
bush, it is my love. Oh, you treach-'rous au - tumn

ne - ro, ha se - ca do mi ro - sal. Ca - rre
wea-ther that has killed my lit - tle tre. Oh, you
ne - ro, tu ca - ri - ño_en-ga - ña-
wea-ther, oh you dear un - faith - ful

dor. *(hablado)* Así cantó la charerita. ¿Cuándo? Ha-ce_un ra-
one. (spoken) So sang the farmer girl. When? A mo - ment

4

Carretero, carretero,
te llevaste mi querer.
Carretero, carretero,
para nunca más volver,
que no has de volver si es cierto,
carretero como hay ser,
donde una esperanza ha muerto,
otra hay volver a nacer.
Así cantaba la chacarerita
¿Cuándo?   *Chorus*

Oh, you cartman, oh, you cartman,
You have carried off my heart.
Oh, you cartman, oh, you cartman,
Nevermore I'll see your cart.
If it's sure that you won't come back,
Then I guess it has to be,
But where one fond hope lies dying,
Then another one I'll see.
So sang the farmer-girl.
When?   *Chorus*

El Carretero
The Cartman

Guitar Solo

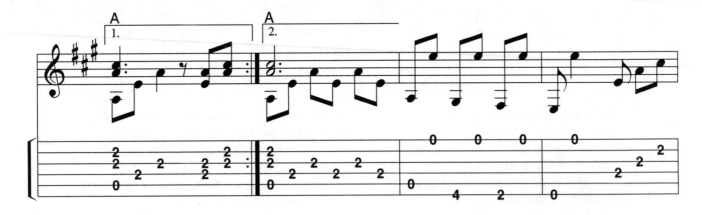

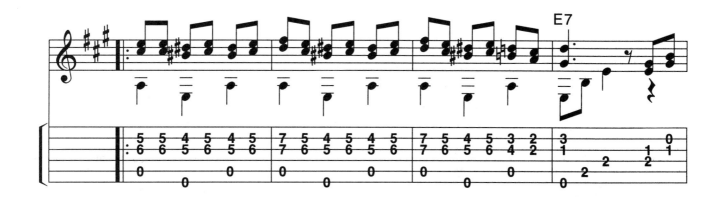

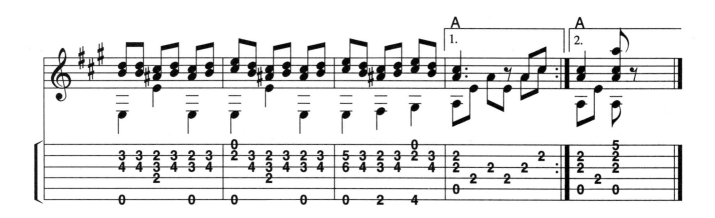

Vidalita
My Little Life

This lively, bouncing dance is reminiscent of the Polish mazurka. Much of Argentinean culture has always had a decidedly European cast.

Argentina - Song and Accompaniment

Vidala

Des - de que te fuis - / Since you went a - way,

te, mi_a-man-te bien, no hay un dul - ce dí - a. / oh,' my dear-est love, there's not been a sweet day. Pá - li-das las ho - / Col-or-less the hours

ras pa-sar se ven, po - bre suer - te mí - a. / seem to pass me by, cruel fate has come my way. Al - ma de mi al - / Soul-mate of my soul,

ma, la blan-ca flor, que al par-tir me dis - te. / when you went a - way, you gave me a white flow'r. Se do bló_a ba-ti / Now it's droop-ing down,

8

da per dió_el co - lor, va mu - rien - do tris - te.
fad - ing fast a - way, dy - ing in its last hour.
Pá - li - das las ho -
Col - or - less the hours

ras pa - sar se ven, po - bre suer - te mí - a.
seem to pass me by, cruel fate has come my way.

1. Dm
a.

2. Dm
way.

Tanta es la tristeza de mi pesar, tan amargo el llanto,
Que con él regarla fuera a matar la flor de mi encanto.
Vuelve, oh vida, y trae para la flor, agua de la fuente,
A su blando riego, flor del amor, te alzarás sonriente,
Pálidas las horas pasar se ven, pobre suerte mía.

So great is the sorrow, I am weighed down and I weep bitter tears.
As they showered down, their droplets did kill my enchanted white flower.
Come back, o my life, and bring for the flower water from the fountain.
By this gentle rain, flower of my heart, you shall rise up smiling.
And the pallid hours, slowly they pass by, cruel fate has come my way.

Vidalita
My Little Life

Guitar Solo

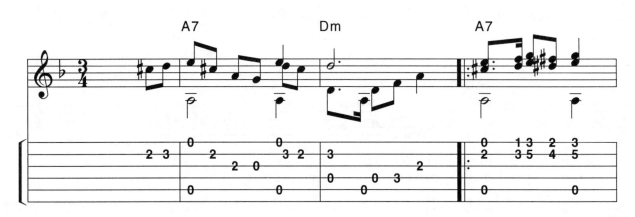

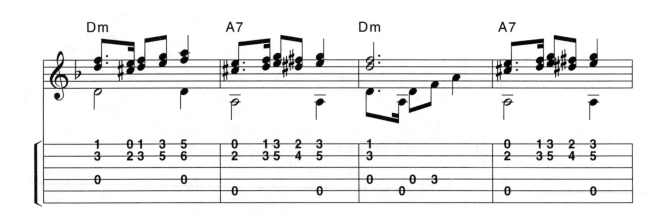

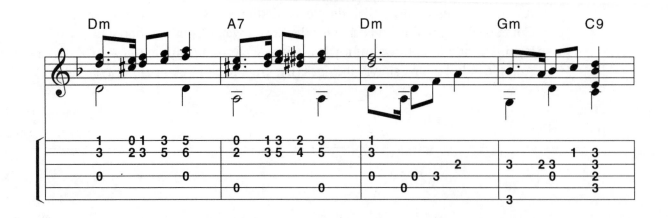

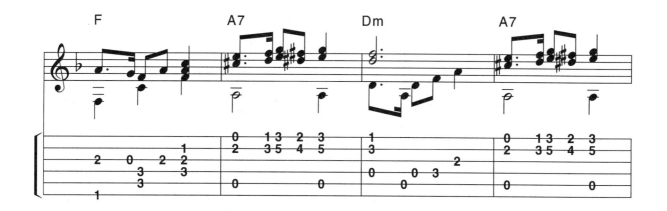

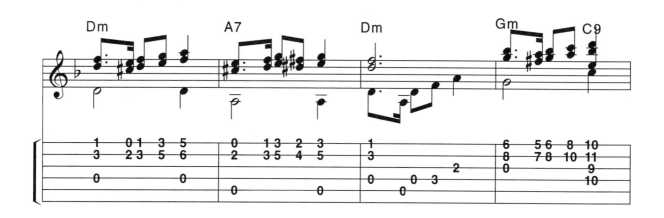

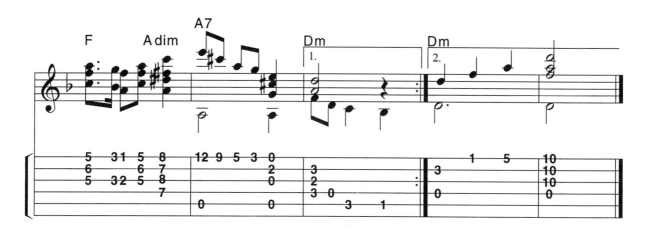

Te Lo Contaré
I'll Tell You All About it

The pentatonic structure of this typical *huaino* clearly points to its Indian origins.

Bolivia Song and Accompaniment

Huaino

Te lo con-ta - ré_a tí pu-
I'll tell you all a - bout it,

es, te lo—— bai - la-ré. A quien más
Then I'll dance it just for you. Whom do you

quie-ras a - sí pues te la—— tra - e - ré.
love the fond-est, I will steal— her a - way.

Calzados bayos para tí,
el taco restares.
De lejos que vean pues
las amistades.

Think you're so smart in your brown shoes,
You'll be down at the heel.
From far off all your friends can see
Just the way you do feel.

Te Lo Contaré
I'II Tell You All About it

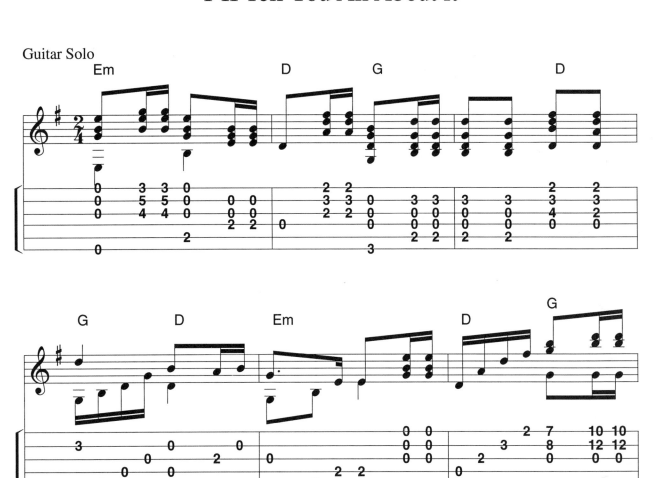

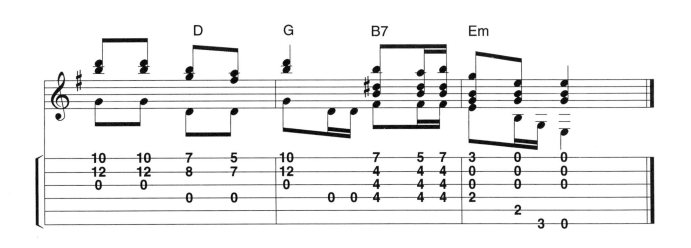

Calla, No Llores
Hush, Don't Cry

Yaravi is a word in the Guarani Indian language. It is a dance form.

Bolivia Song and Accompaniment

Yaravi

E - res pa - ra mí más dul - ce que_el recuer - do de la_in -
To me you are so much sweet - er than the re - mem-brance of

fan - cia. Ca - lla, no llo - res co - ra - zón.
child-hood. O hush, and don't you cry, my heart.

En tu_alien - to_hay más fra - gan - cia que per-fu -
And in your breath there's more fra - grance than the per -

me_en ca - da flor. Ca - lla, no llo - res co - ra -
fume of each flow'r. O hush, and don't you cry my

14

Calla, No Llores
Hush, Don't Cry

Tutú Marambá

If the baby doesn't fall asleep, the evil spirit *Tutú Marambá* will come and eat it. Not exactly a soothing bedtime story, but think of all the scary Mother Goose and Grimm fairy tales you heard as a child. To make matters even worse, the spider, *Aranha Tatanha* ("aranya tatanya") is also keeping his eye on things in company with *Tatú*, the armadillo.

Brazil Song and Accompaniment

Tutú Marambá

Guitar Solo

Morena, Morena

Morena is the dark-complexioned woman, whose beauty runs like a thread through many Latin American songs. The word itself derives from "moor" (as in "Othello, the Moor of Venice").

Brazil Song and Accompaniment

Mo-re-na, Mo-re-na, teus o-lhos cas-
Mo-re-na, Mo-re-na, your eyes brown as

ta - nhos, teus o-lhos bri-lhan - tes são dois di - a -
chest-nuts, your bril-liant eyes shin - ing. are bright as two

man - tes. Mo-re-na, Mo-re - na, Mo-re-na, Mo-
dia - monds.

re - na,   Mo-re-na,   Mo - re - na,   tem pe - na   de
                                                        have pi - ty   on

mim.   Mo-re-na, Mo -   tem pe-na   de mim.
me.   have pi-ty on me.

Morena, Morena

Guitar Solo

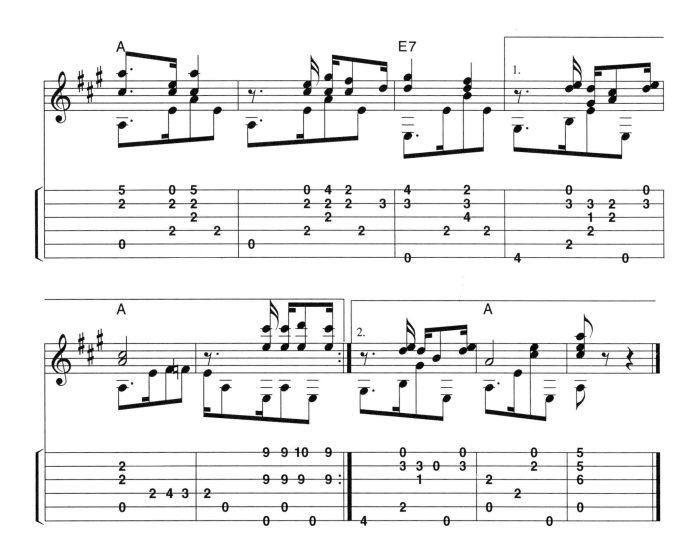

Mi Caballo Blanco
My White Horse

Chile   Song and Accompaniment

Mi ca- ba- llo,   mi ca - ba- llo,   se va   y_se va.   Ah, ———
My faith- ful horse,   My faith- ful horse,   Goes on   and on.

Ah, ——— Ah, ——— Ah,   Ah. ———

harmonic 12

En alas de una dicha
Mi caballo corrió.
Y en brazos de una pena
También él me llevó. *Chorus*

Hasta que a Dios le pido
Que lo tenga muy bien,
Si a su lado me llama
En mi blanquito iré. *Chorus*

Riding on wings of gladness,
My white horse carried me.
And in the arms of sadness,
Together we shall be. *Chorus*

I ask the Lord to keep him,
Safe - and to be his guide.
And when the Lord shall call me,
On Whitey I shall ride. *Chorus*

Mi Caballo Blanco
My White Horse

Guitar Solo

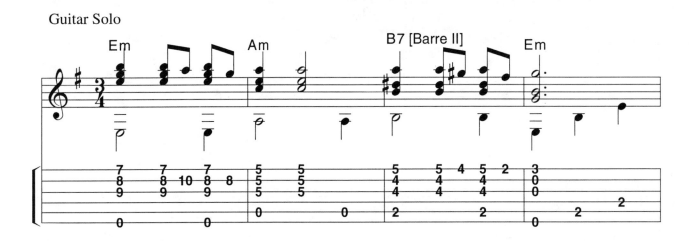

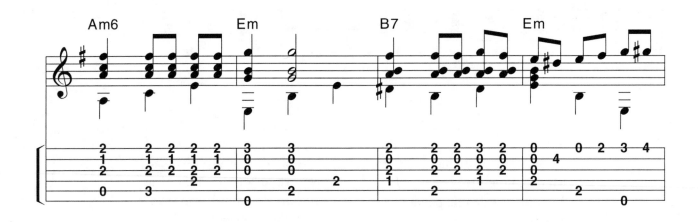

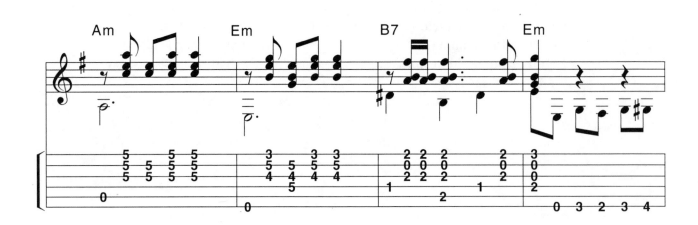

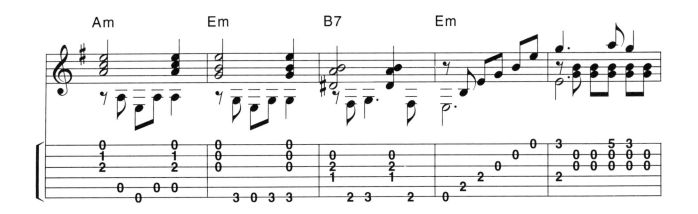

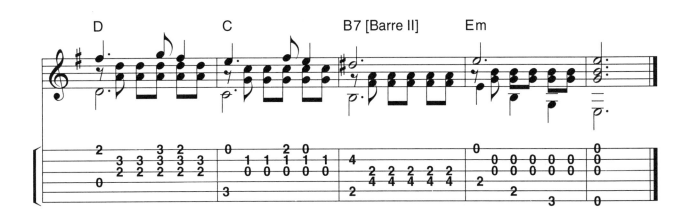

Ámame Mucho
Love Me As Much
(As I Love You)

A typical *cueca* presents contrasting metrical sections: a heavily accented introduction (and interlude) in "three," and the main body of the song in "six."

Chile Song and Accompaniment

llá_en la no-che ca - lla-da pa-ra que se_oi - ga me-jor,_____ Á-ma-me
off in the qui-et   night so it can be   heard much bet-ter,_____ Love me as

3/12 = 3rd string, 12th fret; 5/10 = 5th string, 10th fret... etc.

30

Ámame Mucho
Love Me As Much
(As I Love You)

Guitar Solo

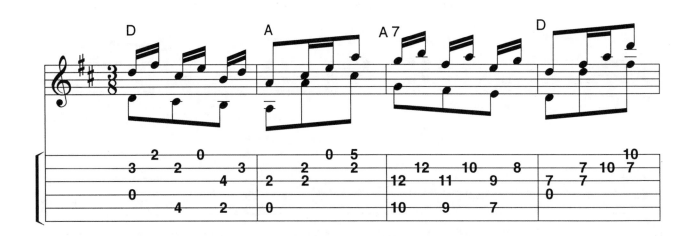

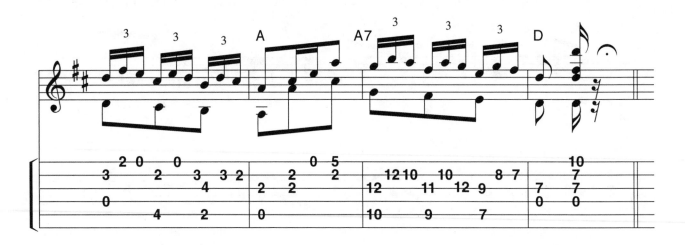

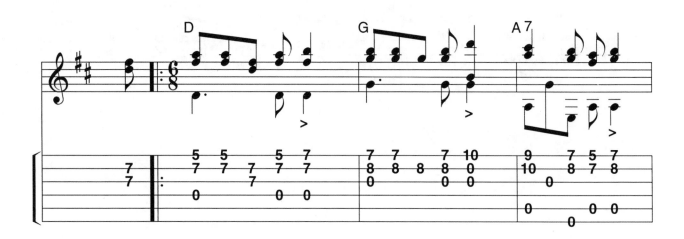

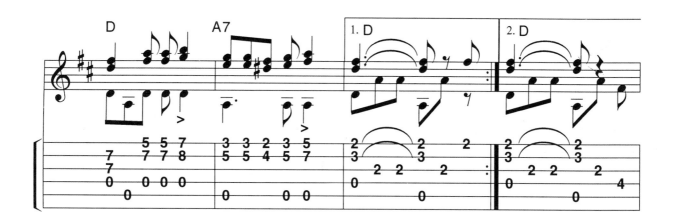

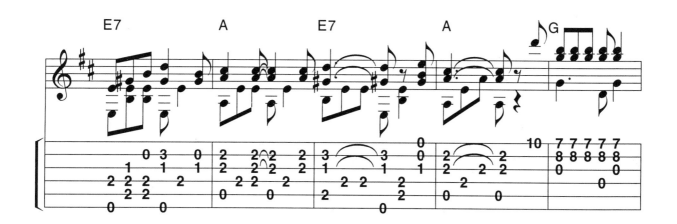

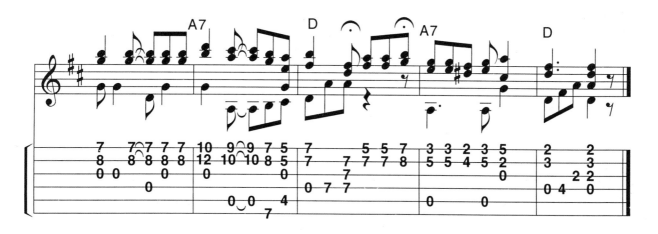

El Zancudo
The Mosquito

Colombia Song and Accompaniment

Pa matar ese animal
Se tendió l'infantería
Con quince ametralladoras
Y un cañón d'infantería.
    La carne d'este animal
    La mandaron pa Marmato
    Pesaba dos mil arrobas,
    Catorce libros y cuarto.

El sebo d'este animal
Lo mandaron p'al Tabor.
Eso hace quinientos años
Y todavía hay jabón.
    Del cuero d'ese animal
    Salieron dos mil paraguas,
    Y un pedazo que sobró
    Se lu'hizo una vieja en naguas.

In order to kill this monster,
The army, it had to be called up,
With fifteen machine guns blazing -
A cannon was also rolled up.
    The flesh of this great mosquito
    Was sent off to feed Marmato.
    Five thousand pounds it did weigh,
    Plus forty more pounds and a quarter.

The fat of this great mosquito
Was sent over to Tabor.
That was five hundred years ago -
Of soap, they still need no more.
    The hide yielded up two thousand
    Umbrellas for rainy weather.
    And from the small piece left over,
    A fine skirt was stitched together.

El Zancudo
The Mosquito

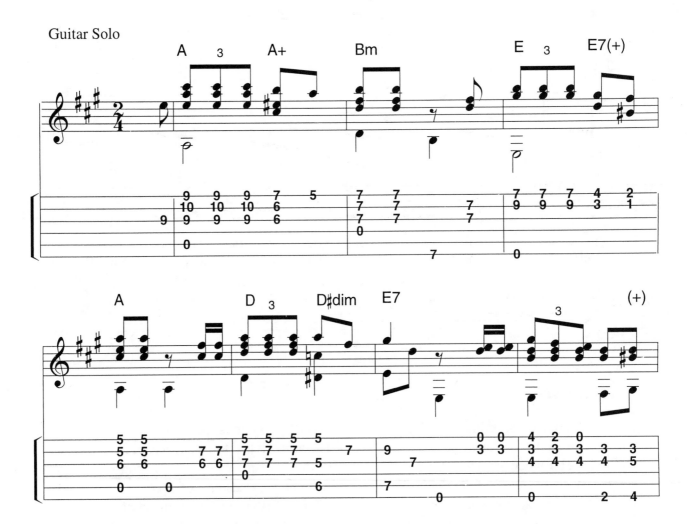

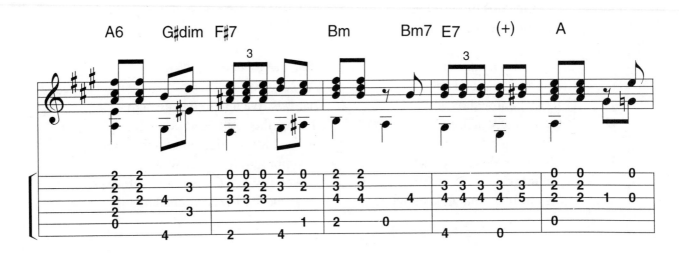

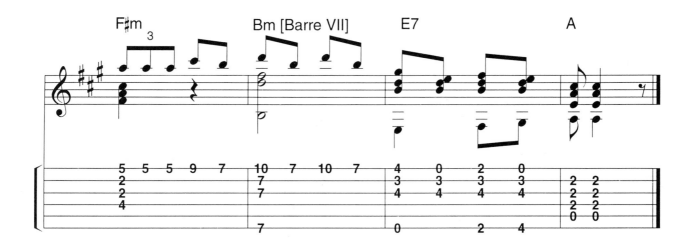

Van Cantando Por La Sierra
O'er The Mountain They Go Singing

Colombia Song and Accompaniment

Canta el ave enamorada
En el follaje sombrío,
Y murmura en la enramada
Su extraño lenguaje al río.

Se escucha el suave concierto
De hojarascas y bejucos,
Mientras que se lleva el viento
El eco de mis bambucos.

And the lovesick bird is singing,
As the somber leaves do quiver;
How it murmurs in the branches,
In its language, by the river.

Gentle sounds are heard all mingled,
Of the dried leaves and lianas,
While the rising wind does carry
The echo of my *bambucos.* *

               * bambuco, a dance

Van Cantando Por La Sierra
O'er The Mountain They Go Singing

Guitar Solo

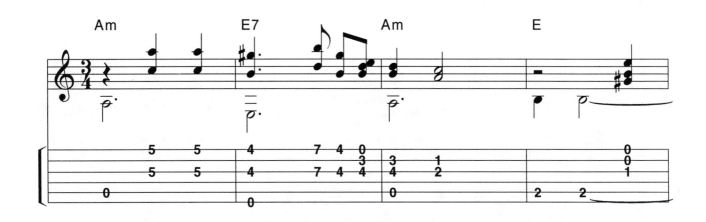

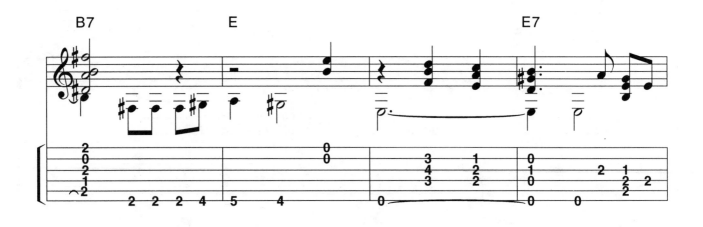

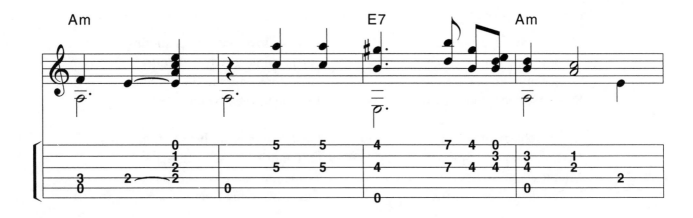

¡Ay! Tituy

Costa Rica   Song and Accompaniment

Fine

La pie- dra que mu- cho rue- da ——
The stone that keeps on a- roll- ing,——

Fine

Em   A7

no sir- ve pa- ra ci- mien- to ——— como_el hom- bre —— sin ver- güen- za
Won't make a sol- id foun- da- tion. ——— Like the man who —— loves the la- dies, But

1. D   2. D

que no tra- ta de ca- sa- mien- to. ——— La mien- to. ¡Ay! ti-
who shuns mar- riag- e's com- pli- ca- tion. —— The ca- tion.

To Chorus

Me dices que no me quieres,	You say that you do not love me,
Porque no te he dado nada	And that I gave you nothing.
Acordate del centavo	Just remember that *centavo*
Que te dí el año pasado. *Chorus*	That I gave to you just last spring. *Chorus*
Me dices que no me quieres,	You say that you do not love me,
Porque yo te dí mal pago.	Because I paid you poorly.
Volveme a querer de nuevo,	Come back once more and love me -
Porque un clavo saca otro clavo. *Chorus*	One nail drives another surely. *Chorus*

¡Ay! Tituy

Guitar Solo

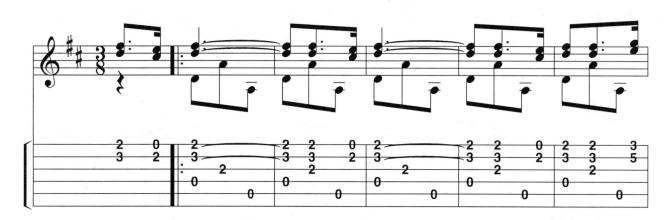

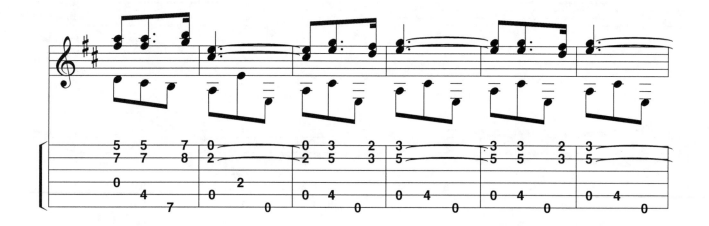

Fine

Fine

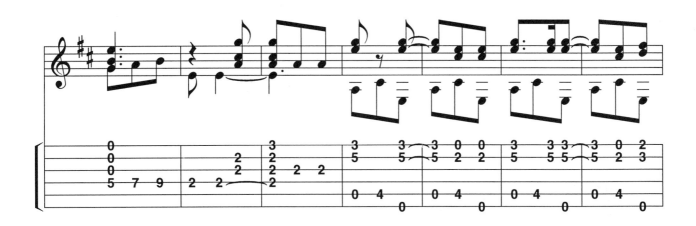

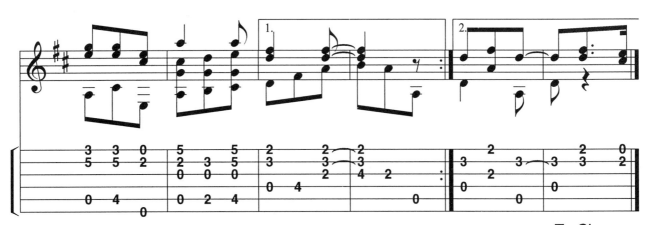

To Chorus

El Toro Pinto
The Spotted Bull

Costa Rica Song and Accompaniment

Si ese toro me matare,	And if this brave bull does kill me,
No me entierren en sagrado.	Don't bury me in the churchyard,
Entiérrenme en campo afuera,	Just lay my bones on the prairie,
Donde me pise el ganado. *Chorus*	Where cattle will trample on me. *Chorus*
No murió de calentura,	He didn't die of a fever,
Ni de dolor al costado;	Nor of some pain in his body,
Murió de una cornada	But rather a vicious goring;
Que le dió el toro pintado. *Chorus*	The bull left him lying bloody. *Chorus*
Allá en aquél rincón	And in some forgotten corner,
Pintado de colorado,	Now reddened by his blood flowing,
Allí están las cinco letras	There marked by a plain inscription,
Donde murió el desdichado. *Chorus*	Died the unlucky bullfighter. *Chorus*

El Toro Pinto
The Spotted Bull

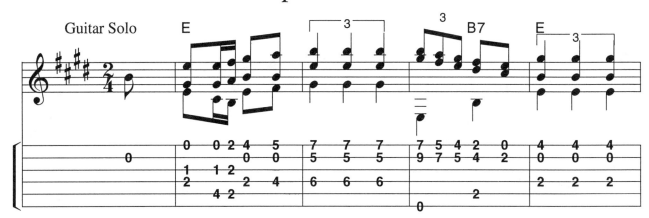

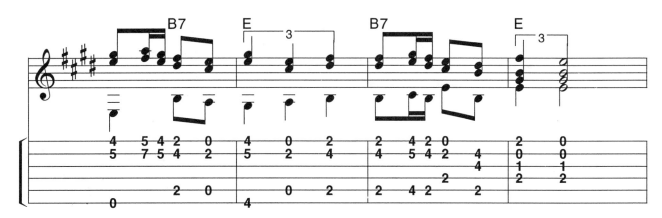

Bañado El Rostro
Bathed Was Her Fair Face

The infectious rhythm of the *habanera* may be heard as the accompaniment to songs and dances all over Latin America. Perhaps the most famous *habanera* was composed by a Frenchman (Bizet) to be sung by a Spanish gypsy (Carmen).

Cuba Song and Accompaniment   Habanera

Ba - ña-do_el ros- tro,_____ En luz di - vi - na,
Bathed was her fair face_____ in light ce - les - tial,

Cán - di-da_y pu - ra,_____ be - lla_y a - sí._____ Co-mo_es - as
In - no-cent, pure, a_____ beau-ty to see._____ As with these

co - sas_____ que son de cie - lo_____ u - na ma - ñ - na
things that_____ come down from hea - ven_____ one ear - ly morn - ing

la co - no - cí. E - ra tan pu - ra_____ la ne - gra
she came to me. It was so dark then,_____ When night de -

48

Bañado El Rostro
Bathed Was Her Fair Face

Guitar Solo

La Tarde
The Evening

Although the *bolero* is of Spanish origin, and here transported to Cuba, as with the *"Bizet-habanera* connection," it remained for another French composer, Maurice Ravel, to write the *bolero* that has come to symbolize this dance all over the world.

Cuba Song and Accompaniment   Bolero

La Tarde
The Evening

Guitar Solo

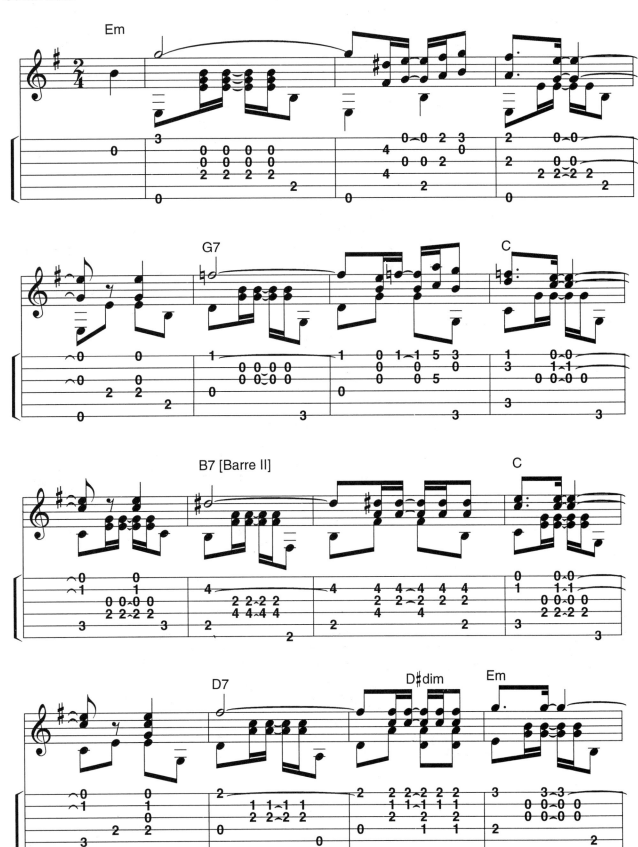

57

Tomá Juyó
Tomás Ran Away

This is the earliest known *merengue,* the dance that has become the "national dance" of the Dominican Republic. It dates from the Battle of Talanquera, in 1844, between opposing Dominican and Haitian soldiers. Under Haitian attack, a certain Tomás Torres abandoned his station, fleeing with the Dominican flag. Eventually the Dominican troops counterattacked and won the day. Soon after the battle, Dominican soldiers began singing and dancing this song, ridiculing the cowardly behavior of the runaway Torres.

As with most new forms of popular music (think of ragtime, jazz and rock 'n' roll in our own country), the Dominican musical "establishment" started out by being virulently anti-*merengue*. Poems were written in outrage with lines like *el torpe merengue aborrecible* (the crude and despicable *merengue),* and *hijo digno del diablo y de una furia...tú villano, que insultas al pudor* (true son of the devil and a fury...you villain, who insults chastity). But the *merengue* (like ragtime, etc.) hung on and had the last laugh.

Dominican Republic   Song and Accompaniment   Merengue

Tomá Juyó
Tomás Ran Away

Duérmete, Mi Niño
Sleep, My Child

This tender lullaby originated in Spain, and is sung in a number of other Latin American countries including the Dominican Republic

Dominican Republic Song and Accompaniment

Duér - me-te, mi ni - ño, Duér - me-te, mi_a - mor,_____
Sleep, my lit - tle ba - by, Sleep, my lit - tle dove,_____

Duer - me dul - ce_en - can - to de mi co - ra - zón._____
Sleep, you sweet en - chant - ment of your moth - er's love._____

Ay, mi Palomita,	O my little pigeon,
la que yo adoré,	One that I adored,
que nació allá	Born so far away,
y voló se fue.	Will return no more.
Ella no comía	It would never eat food,
ni trigo ni arroz,	Neither rice nor wheat;
y se mantenía	All it ever needed,
sólo con amor.	Was my love so sweet.

Repeat first verse

Duérmete, Mi Niño
Sleep, My Child

Guitar Solo

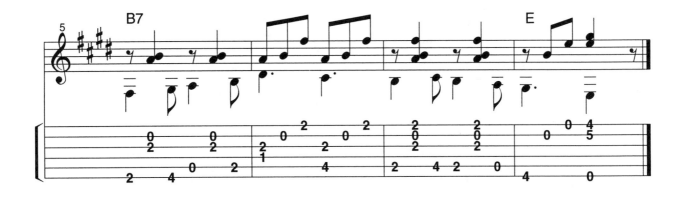

Kurikinga

A *kurikinga* is a bird. In this context it is applied to a lively, vivacious woman.

Ecuador Song and Accompaniment

Ku - ri - kin - ga, ma - pa - ña - wi, Ku - ri - kin - ga, ma - pa -
Ku - ri - kin - ga, two - faced wo - man, Ku - ri - kin - ga, two - faced

ña - wi, Da la me - dia vuel - ta, Ku - ri - kin - ga, Da la vuelta_en - ter - a, Ku - ri -
wo man. Swing half way a - round now, Ku - ri - kin - ga, Swing around and 'round now, Ku - ri -

kin - ga, Me - nea que me - ne - a, Ku - ri - kin - ga, Be - be la co - pi - ta, Ku - ri -
kin - ga, shake it ba - by, shake it Ku - ri - kin - ga, Drink a lit - tle whis - ky, Ku - ri -

kin - ga, Has - ta que te can - ses, Ku - ri - kin - ga. Ku - ri - kin - ga, ma - pa -
kin - ga, It will make you fris - ky, Ku - ri - kin - ga. Ku - ri - kin - ga, two - faced

ña - wi, Ku - ri - kin - ga, ma - pa - ña - wi, Da la me dia vuel - ta, Ku - ri - kin - ga.
woman, Ku - ri - kin - ga, two - faced woman. Swing half way a - round now, Ku - ri - kin - ga.

Kurikinga

Guitar Solo

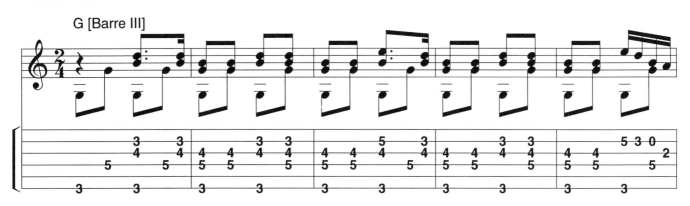

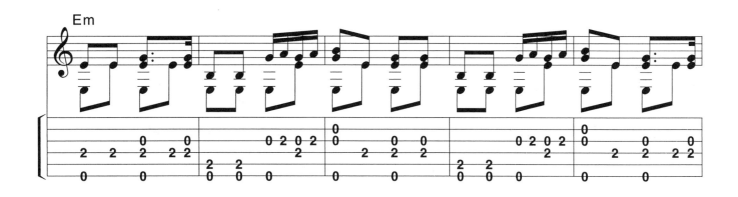

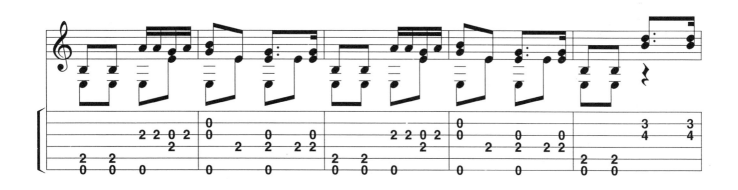

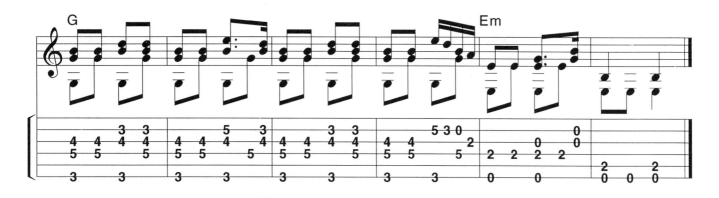

Separación
Separation

The Christianized Indians of the Andes adopted many saints as their own. San Juan (St. John) is, perhaps, their favorite. A *sanjuanito* is dance performed before the many shrines erected in that saint's honor.

Ecuador Song and Accompaniment

Sanjuanito

Mi ma-dre me_ha di-cho no de-bes llo-rar, Mi ma-dre me_ha di-cho no
My moth-er did tell me that I shouldn't cry, My moth-er did tell me that

de-bes llo-rar, Llo-rar por los muer-tos, por los que se van, Llo-
I should-n't cry, For those who are gone, And for those who did die, For

rar por los muer-tos por los que se van.
those who are gone, And for those who did die.

To-rren-te de lá-gri-mas a mí me cos-tó, To-rren-te de lá-gri-mas a
A tor-rent of bit-ter tears I was forced to shed, A tor-rent of bit-ter tears I

64

mí me cos - tó,   Sa - lir   de mi tie - rra don - de na - cí yo,   Sa-
wasforced to   shed,   To   part   from the land where I   was born and bred,   To

lir de mi tie - rra don - de na - cí yo.   *Fine*
part fromthe land where I   was born and bred.

Fine

Tris - te muy tris - te la se-pa-ra-ción,   Tris-te muy tris-te la se-pa-ra-ción,
Sad se-pa - ra-tion, It's hard to de-part,   Sad se-pa - ra-tion, It's hard to de-part,

Por que_en au - sen - cia se guar-da pa - sión,   Por que_en au-sen - cia se guar- da pa - sión.
Leav - ing   the land that is   dear to my heart,   Leav - ing the land that is dear   to my heart.

D.S. al Fine

Separación
Separation

Guitar Solo

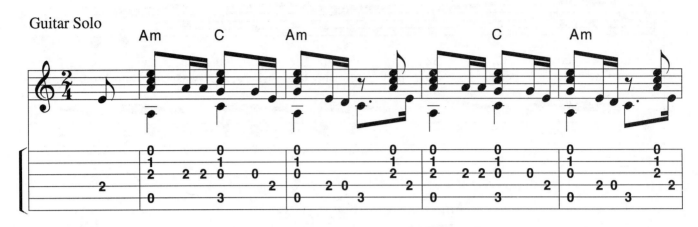

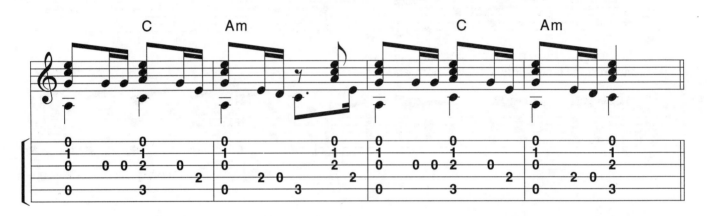

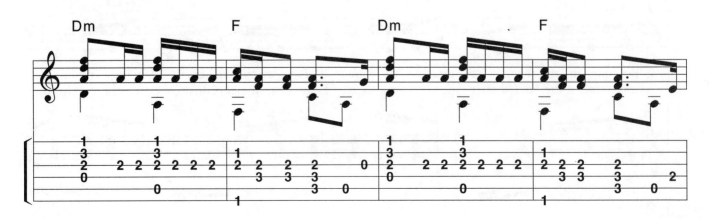

Fine

Fine

D. S. al Fine

Vamos A La Mar
Let's Go To The Sea

Guatemala   Song and Accompaniment

Va - mos a la mar, tum tum, A co - mer pes -
Let's go to the sea, tum tum, And we'll eat some

ca - do, tum tum. Bo - ca co - lo - ra - da, tum
fish there, tum tum. Eat them fried or roast - ed, tum

tum, Fri - ti - to_y a - sa - do, tum tum.
tum, What a tast - y dish there, tum tum.

Vamos a la mar, tum tum,	Let's go to the sea, tum tum,
A comer pescado, tum tum,	Any way you do it, tum tum,
Frito y asado, tum tum,	Eat them fried or roasted, tum tum,
En sartén de palo, tum tum.	Or you barbecue it, tum tum.

Vamos A La Mar
Let's Go To The Sea

Guitar Solo

Nací En La Cumbre
I Was Born On The Mountain

Guatemala Song and Accompaniment

Unos bandidos me alimentaron,	Well, I was fed by a band of outlaws,
A la cuitada que me dio el ser;	And the poor woman who gave me birth,
Hijo del Trueno me apellidaron,	They all did call me the son of Thunder,
Y en noche obscura vine a nacer.	Since that dark night - my first on earth.
Si tú no sales a tu ventana,	If you don't come to your bedroom window,
Perla de Oriente, nítida flor,	Pearl of the Orient, my pretty flower,
Cabe tus muros verás mañana	Against your wall you will see tomorrow,
Rota mi lira, muerto al cantor.	The broken lyre of my final hour.

Nací En La Cumbre
I Was Born On The Mountain

Guitar Solo

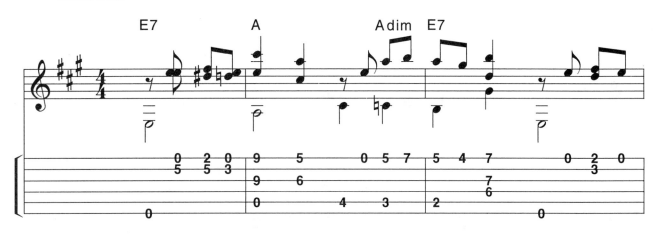

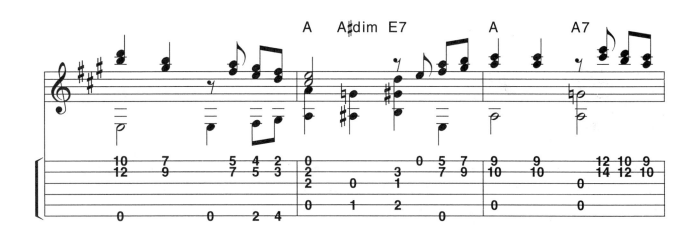

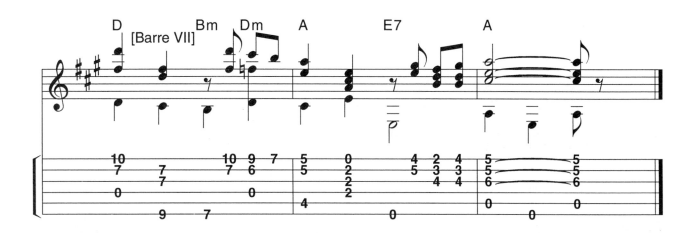

Les Emigrés
The Emigrants

Haitian *emigrés* coming to New York in the early 1930s faced the usual discrimination accorded most black immigrants. Their unfortunate situation was exacerbated by the Depression. Nevertheless, a ray of hope still shines through this song.

Haiti Song and Accompaniment

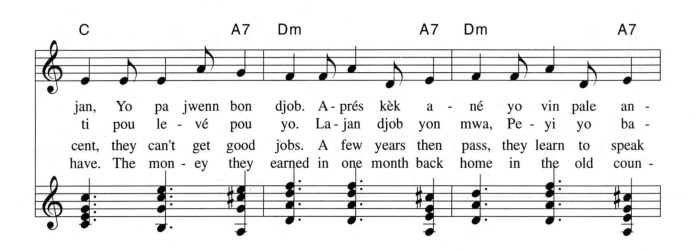

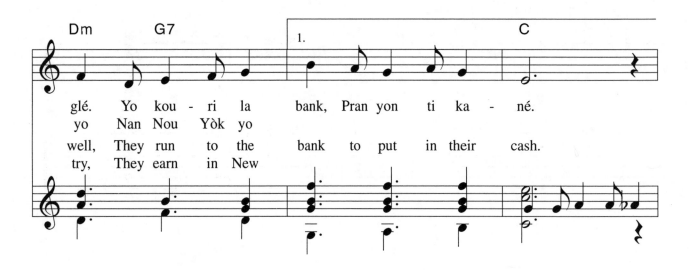

Nou Yòk se yon vil
Ki pa kab konté
Diferan peplad
Ki groupé ladan'l.
Kanta bél medam,
Ranpli detiket.
Yo sanble ti zanj
Ki soti nan syel.
Lóganizasyon
Vi Nou Yòk la
Fe tout moun maché
Na dwa chemen.
An deyò de sa,
Nou jwenn tout bagay,
Mwen pa kwe Leròp
Kapab fe pou nou. *Chorus*

New York is a town
Which just cannot count
The different groups
Of people here found.
Its women are beauties,
And have great charm.
They are just like angels
Down from the skies.
The way life is run
Right here in New York,
Makes every man
Just stick to his work.
And what's even more,
There's so much around,
I don't think Europe
Could do more for us. *Chorus*

Chorus 2:
Devan yon dousè parèy,
Yo fe yo Ameriken,
Pou yo siveyé
Leurs propres intérêts
Se pa yon dezoné,
Se pa yon lacheté,
Se to simpman
Yon devwa yo ranpli.

Chorus 2:
Because of such good luck,
They become citizens,
In order to protect
Their proper interests.
It's not a dishonor,
It is not cowardice.
It's simply a matter
Of doing what must be done.

Si w rivé Nou Yòk ,
Lo w fin pale anglé,
Ou pa fè lanjan,
S'on krim w ap peyé.
Kar nenpòt nasyon
Ki rantre Nou Yòk.
Apre kèk ané,
Li tounen Kresus
Avan kèk ané,
Li gentan maryé.
La pe banboché
Avek madanm li.
Li vin gen oto,
Li vin gen bilding,
Si nou kwè'm manti,
Al mande Jwif yo.

So when you get here,
And English you learn,
If you don't do well,
It would be a crime.
For any nation
That comes to New York,
After a few years
Becomes like Croesus.
And then pretty soon
They all get married,
Enjoy a good life
With their darling wife.
Then they buy a car,
Then buy a building.
If you think I'm lying,
Go ask the Jews.

Chorus 3:
Nou zòt pitit Etiopi,
Lè nou rivé bo la,
Sa réd pou nou jwenn yon rout.
Nou tonbé an derout.
Nou mèt tann nwit kon jou,
Chemen baré pou nou.
Se yon dezespwa
Pou nom ki gen po nwa.

Chorus 3:
But we Ethiopian sons,
When we come to these shores,
It's hard to find the path,
And so we often fail.
Though we wait nights and days,
The road is blocked for us.
A hopeless condition
For him who's born with black skin.

Les Emigrés
The Emigrants

Guitar Solo

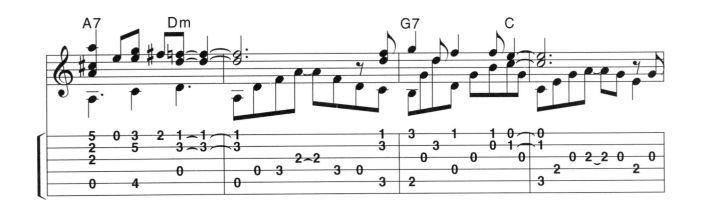

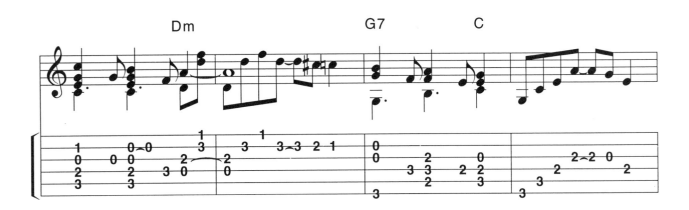

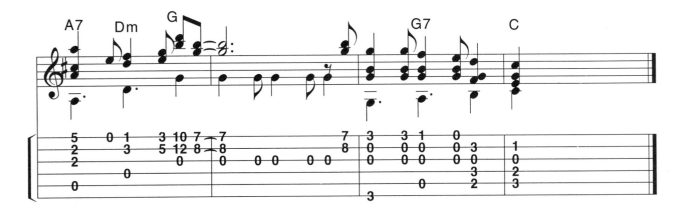

Feuille-o
Leaves-o

The distraught mother calls out to the spirit of the leaves, *feuille-o* ("feyo") to save the life of her sick child. The *gan-gan* is the witch doctor or medicine man.

Haiti Song and Accompaniment

Feuille - o, — sau-vez la vie moin, — nan mi - ser moin ye -
Leaves - o, — won't you save my life, — won't you end my suf -

o.
fring?

o.
fring?

Pi - tit moin ma-lade, m' cou - ri
O, my child is sick, I'll run to

caille gan-gan, si - mi - lo. _____
the gan-gan, Hear my cry. _____

2nd. time Si li
And a

Pi - tit bon gan-gan, la sau-vez
O, my good gan-gan, will save my

la vie moin, nan mi - ser moin ye o.
life, I know, He will end my suf - fring.

Feuille-o
Leaves-o

Guitar Solo

79

Flores De Mimé
Flowers of Mimé

Honduras Song and Accompaniment

A la_o - ri - lla del rí - o Ver - be - na de
On the banks of the *rí - o Ver - be - na de*

Ma - ro - mé, flo - res de mi - mé. Ten -
Ma - ro - mé, Bright mi - mé flow - ers, There

go sem - bra - do a - za -
I have plant - ed cin - na -

frán y ca-ne - la, ver - be - na, de Ma - ro - mé, flo - res
mon, saf - fron and some ver - be - na, In Ma - ro - mé, bright *mi -*

de mi - mé, Pi - mien - ta_y cla - vo.——
mé flow - ers, And pep - pers and cloves.——

En la falda de la montaña	In the foothills of yonder high mountain
De Maromé, flores de mimé.	In Maromé. bright *mimé* flowers,
Están sembrando	They are all planting
Un yucal, un cañal y canela	Cinnamon, saffron and some verbena,
De Maromé, flores de mimé,	In Maromé, bright *mimé* flowers,
Y maíz morado.	And purple sweet corn.
Cuando quiero cantarle a mi chata	When I want to sing to my .sweetheart,
De Maromé, flores de mimé,	In Maromé. bright *mimé* flowers,
Con mi guitarra,	I take my guitar,
Ensillo mi caballo plateado,	Then I saddle my silver-gray pony,
De Maromé, flores de mimé,	In Maromé. bright *mimé* flowers,
Y voy montado.	And off I gallop.

Repeat first verse

Flores De Mimé
Flowers of Mimé

D7

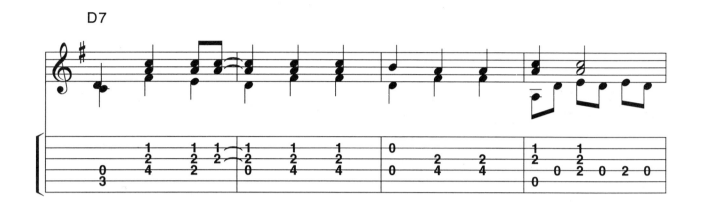

G Am Cm6 D7 G Am

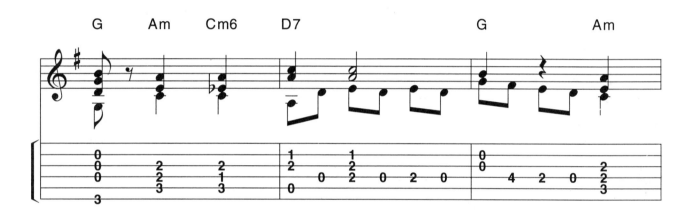

G D7 G

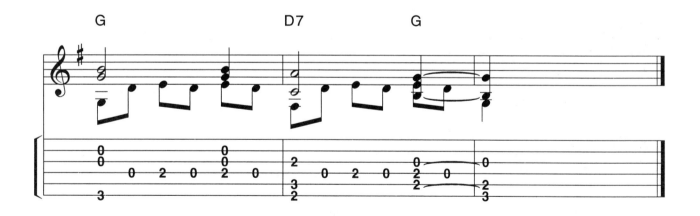

83

Papanulan

Honduras Song and Accompaniment

Pa - pa - nu - lan, Pa - pa - nu - lan, Tra - ba - jan - do_el dí - a
Pa - pa - nu - lan, Pa - pa - nu - lan, Night and day you'll find me

no - che,   ¡Ay! Pa - pa - nu - lan, Pa - pa -
work - ing.   O! Pa - pa - nu - lan, Pa - pa -

nu - lan, Vi - da mí - a._____ Tra - ba - jan - do el_dí - a
nu - lan, My dear sweet - heart._____ Night and day you'll find me

no - che, Ga - nan - cio cua - ren - ta pe - sos.
work - ing, I earn on - ly for - ty pe - sos.

¡Ay! Pa - pa - nu - - - - - lan, - Pa - pa -
O! Pa - pa - nu - - - - - lan, - Pa - pa -

D

nu - lan, vi - da mí - a.
nu - lan, my dear sweet - heart.

Trabajando el día noche,
Ganancio cuarenta peso,
¡Ay! Papanulan,
Trabajando el día noche.

Papanulan, Papanulan,
Papanulan, vida mia,
Quiero que si me astumba
Me alegre tamburira.

Night and day you'll find me working,
I earn only forty pesos,
O! Papanulan,
Night and day you'll find me working.

Papanulan, Papanulan,
Papanulan, my dear sweetheart,
I would like that when I'm buried,
You will beat the drum so gaily.

Papanulan

Guitar Solo

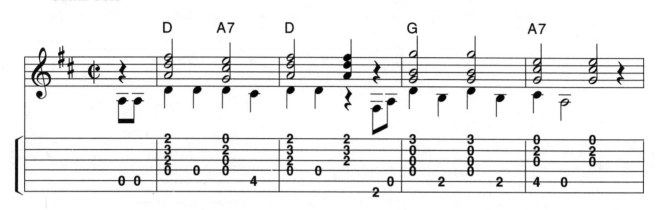

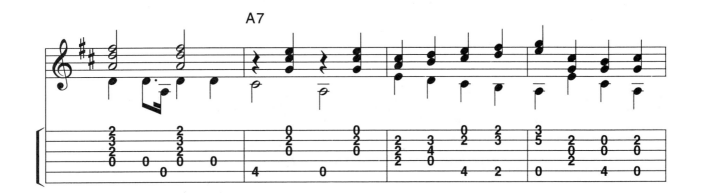

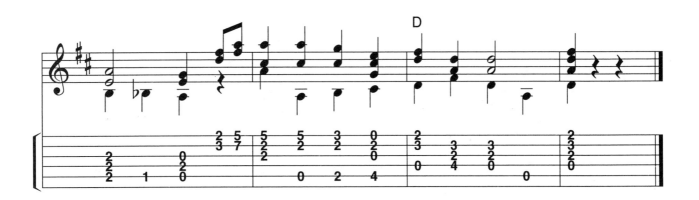

La Llorona
The Weeping Woman

Llorona is often pictured in song as weeping for her dead husband or children. In this love song version, *llorona* is used as a simple refrain.

México   Song and Accompaniment

To - dos me di - cen el ne - gro, Llo - ro - na, ne - gro pe - ro__ ca - ri - ño - so.__ — Yo soy co - mo_el__ chi - le ver - de, Llo - ro - na, pi - can - te pe - ro sa - bro - so.__ Yo — ¡Ay de mi! Llo -

Ev - 'ry one calls me the black one, *Llo - ro - na*, yes, black I am,__ but so lov - ing.__ — I'm like the green__ chi - le pep - per, *Llo - ro - na*, so spic - y but__ o, so tast - y.__ I'm — Woe is me! *Llo -*

88

Dicen que no tengo duelo, llorona,	People say I'm not in mourning, *llorona,*
porque no me ven llorar. (2)	Because they don't see me crying. (2)
Hay muertos que no hacen ruido, llorona,	There are deaths that don't make a sound, *llorona,*
y es más grande su penar. (2)	And whose suffering is so much greater. (2)
Ay de mí, llorona,	Woe is me, *llorona,*
llorona de azul celeste. (2)	*Llorona* of heaven's blue color. (2)
Y aunque la vida me cueste. llorona,	And even if it costs me my life, *llorona,*
no dejaré de quererte. (2)	I will not cease longing for you. (2)
Si al cielo subir pudiera, llorona,	If I could climb up to the heavens, *llorona,*
las estrellas te bajara.(2)	And bring all the stars down before you, (2)
La luna a tus pies pusiera, llorona,	The moon I would place at your feet, o, *llorona,*
con el sol te coronara. (2)	And with the bright sun I would crown you. (2)
Ay de mí, llorona,	Woe is me, *llorona,*
llorona de negros ojos. (2)	*Llorona* of eyes dark as midnight, (2)
Ya con esta se despide,llorona.	And with all this now will be leaving, *llorona,*
tu negrito soñador. (2)	Your little black heartbroken dreamer. (2)

La Llorona
The Weeping Woman

Guitar Solo

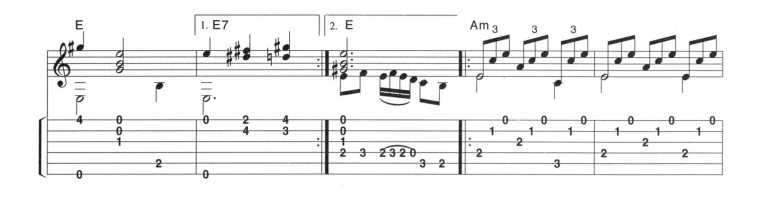

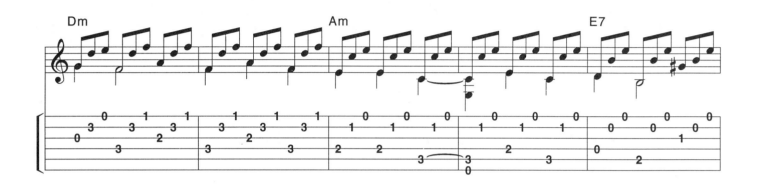

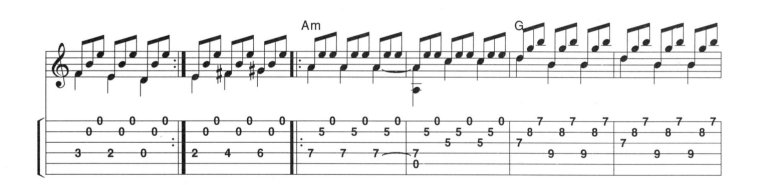

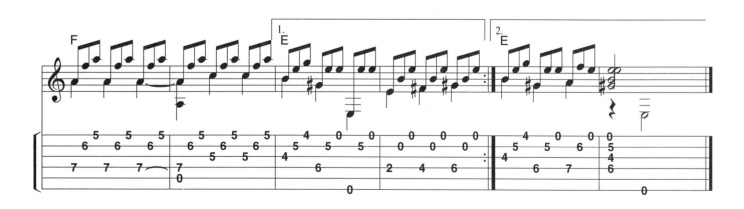

La Malagueña

The original meaning of *La Malagueña* was a woman from Malaga, Spain. It has become widely recognized as a flamenco dance and virtuoso guitar piece. In this song, the meaning is closer to the original, although the woman in question is now Mexican.

México   Song and Accompaniment

falsetto-yodel

sar tus la-bios qui-sie-ra,_____ Ma-la-
yes, kiss your lips with pas-sion,_____ Ma-la-

gue-ña_____ sa-le-ro-sa,_____ y de-cir - te ni-ña_her-mo-sa,_____
gue-ña,_____ o, so charm-ing,_____ And to tell you pret-ty la-dy,_____

e - res lin-da_y he-chi-ce-ra, e - res lin-da_y he-chi -
you are pret-ty and en - chant-ing, you are pret-ty and en -

ce-ra,_____ co-mo_el can-dor de_una ro-sa,_____ y de-cir - te ni-ña_her-mo-sa,_____
chant-ing,_____ As in-no-cent as a rose bud.__ And to tell you, pret-ty la-dy,_____

93

Si por pobre me desprecias,	If for poverty you scorn me,
yo te concedo razón,	I agree you have good reason,
yo te concedo razón	I agree you have good reason,
si por pobre me desprecias.	If for poverty you scorn me.
Yo no te ofrezco riquezas,	I do not offer you riches,
te ofrezco mi corazón,	But I offer you my heart,
te ofrezco mi corazón,	But I offer you my heart,
a cambio de mi pobreza. *Chorus*	In exchange for my poor fortune. *Chorus*

La Malagueña

D.S. al ℁

Hojita De Guarumal
Little Leaf Of The Guarumal

Panamá Song and Accompaniment

Ho - ji - ta de Gua - ru - mal, Don - de
Lit - tle leaf of the gua - ru - mal, That's where

Thumb Down   1st. Finger Up

vi - ve la lan - gos - ta, Don-de co - me, don - de
you can find the lo - cust, And he eats there, And he

duer - me, Don - de vi - ve la lan - gos - ta.
sleeps there, That's where you can find the lo - cust.

Hojita de guarumal,	Little leaf of guarumal,
Donde vive la langosta,	That's where you can find the locust.
Donde come, donde cena,	And he eats there, and he sups there,
Donde duerme la langosta.	That's where you can find him sleeping.
Hojita de guarumal,	Little leaf of the guarumal,
Donde vive la langosta,	That's where you can find the locust.
Donde come, donde toma,	And he eats there, and he drinks there,
Donde duerme la langosta.	That's where you can find him sleeping.
Hojita de guarumal,	Little leaf of guarumal,
Donde vive la langosta,	That's where you can find the locust.
Donde come, donde duerme,	And he eats there, and he sleeps there,
Donde muere la langosta.	That's where he will die, the locust.

Hojita De Guarumal
Little Leaf Of The Guarumal

Guitar Solo

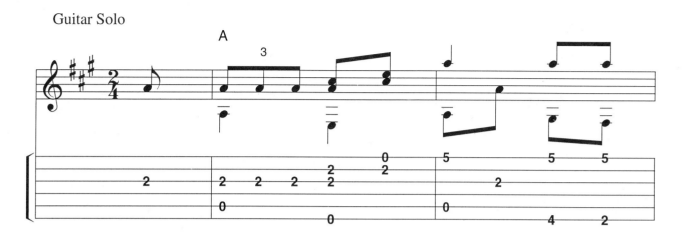

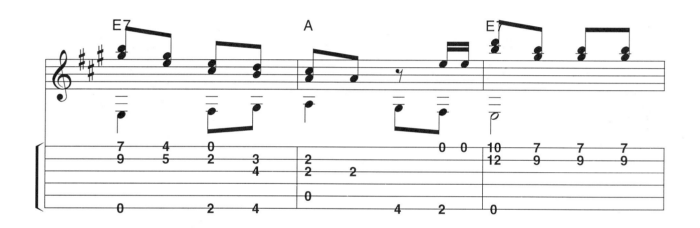

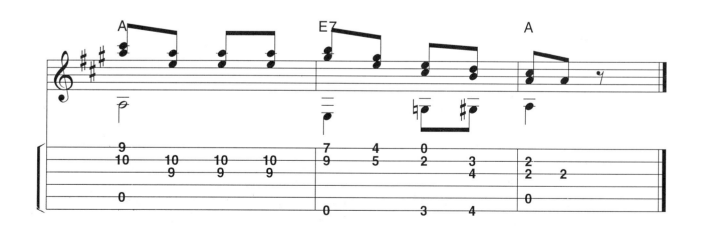

Mi Pollera
My Skirt

Panamá Song and Accompaniment

Mi po - lle - ra, mi po - lle - ra, mi po - lle - ra_es co - lo -
O, my skirt is, o, my skirt is, O, my skirt's a bright red

ra - da. Yo quie - ro_u - na po - lle - ra de_o - lán de co - co, Si tú no me las
co - lor. I'd like to have a skirt made of co - co fi - ber, If you don't give it

das, Me voy con o - tro. Mi po - ti - go.
to me, I will leave you. O, my ev - er

Mi pollera, mi pollera,	O, my skirt is, o, my skirt is,
Mi pollera es colorada.	O, my skirt's a bright red color.
La tuya es blanca, la mía es rosada	That skirt of yours is snow-white and mine is rosy,
Mi pollera es colorada	My skirt is a bright red color.
Mi pollera, mi pollera,	O, my skirt is, o, my skirt is,
Mi pollera es colorada.	O, my skirt's a bright red color.
Yo quiero una pollera de olán de hilo,	I really want a skirt with some fancy trimming,
Si tú me la das, me voy contigo.	And if you give it to me, I'm yours forever.

Mi Pollera
My Skirt

Guitar Solo

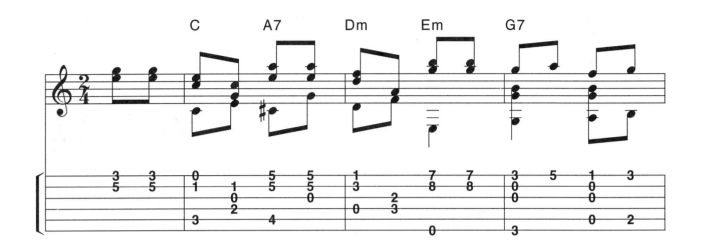

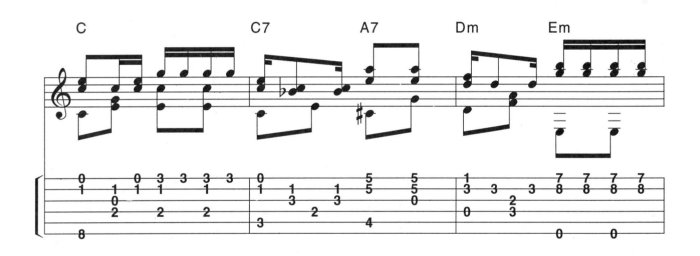

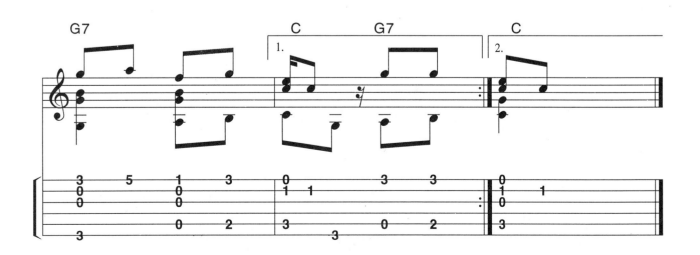

La Guaireñita
The Girl From Guaira

Villarica is the capital of the department of Guaira. A number of words in this song are in the language of the Guaira Indian language: *cuñata-í* means girl; the second line of verse two is translated in the English version; *yboty* means flowers.

Paraguay   Song and Accompaniment

Es Vi - lla - ri - ca u — na vi - lla her - mo - sa,___
Yes Vi - lla - ri - ca's___ a might - y fine town,___

De don - de sur - ge___ cu - ña - ta - î.___
My sweet - heart's from there,___ now don't you see?___

Lle - na de flo - res__ en sus jar - di - nes,___
Cov - ered with flow - ers__ gar - dens full of them,___

¡Vi - va la pa - tria___ del Y - bo - ty!___
Long live the home - land___ of Y - bo - ty!___

Allí yo tengo mi prometida,	That's where she does live, my promised sweetheart,
Yporanüépe na mboyoyai,	The prettiest girl I ever did see;
Como el lucero de la mañana	Just like the bright star that dawns in the morning,
Que anuncia el bello co'embotá.	And that announces a pleasant day.

La Guaireñita
The Girl From Guaira

Guitar Solo

Noches Paraguayas
Paraguayan Evenings

Paraguay - Song and Accompaniment

By Martita Ramirez

Lyrics:

No-ches pa-ra-gua-yas, ___ ba-jo tus es-
Pa-ra-gua-yan evenings, ___ un-der-neathyour

tre-llas, ___ me ha-go mil pre-gun-tas ___
star-light, ___ ask a thous-and questions, ___

en mi so-le-dad; ___ Can-to es-ta güa-
In my sol-i-tude; ___ I sing this güa-

ran-ia, ___ en mis ti-bias no-ches, ___
ran-ia, ___ in my sum-mer eve-nings, ___

a mi_a-mor au - sen - te, _____ que le - jos es -
to my ab - sent lov - er, _____ who is far a -

1.

tá.
way.

2. E7   A

que le- jos es - tá. _____
who is far a - way. _____

Noches paraguayas,
Beso así tu suelo,
Soñando nostalgias
En mi Paraguay.
    Canto esta güarania
    En mis tibias noches,
    A mi amor ausente,
    Que lejos está.

Paraguayan evenings,
Thus I kiss your soil,
Bittersweetly dreaming
In my Paraguay.
    I sing this *güarania*,
    In my summer evenings,
    To my absent lover,
    Who is far away.

Repeat first verse

Noches Paraguayas
Paraguayan Evenings

Guitar Solo

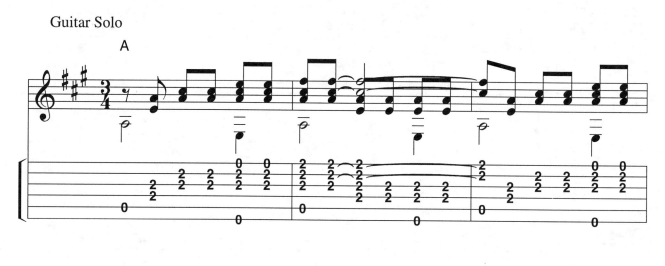

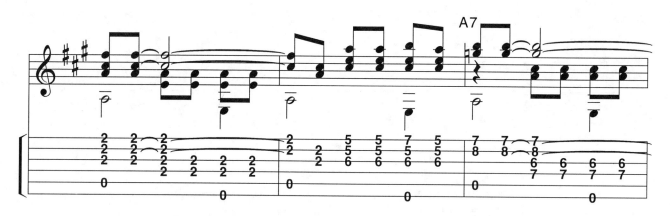

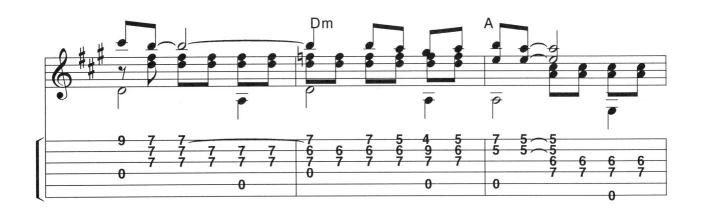

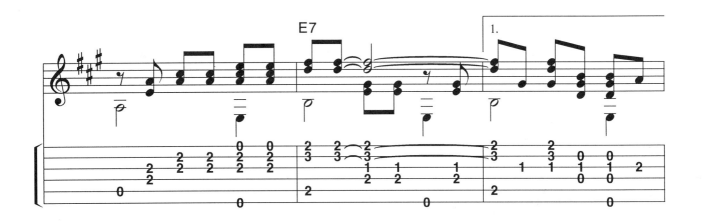

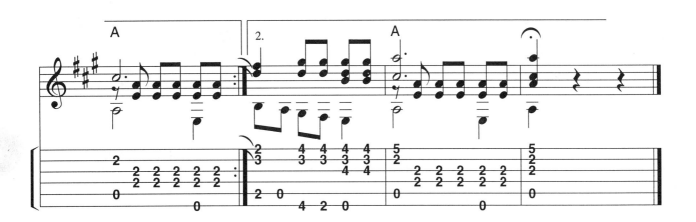

Llanto Del Indio
Lament Of The Indian

Atahualpa was the last Inca ruler. He was defeated by the Spaniards in 1532. Sigalpa was one of his brave generals.

Perú Song and Accompaniment   Yaraví

So - mos los in - dios ro - jos puro_At - a -
We are the red - skinned In - dians of At - a -

hual - pa,_____
hual - pa,_____

Que_en nues - tra_a -
And in our

tri - ción so - mos co - mo Si - gal - pa._____
sad - ness we are just like Si - gal - pa._____

Cuan - do la
And when the

108

lu - na sa - le des - de_el o - rien - te,_____
moon ap - pears in the east - ern heav - ens,_____

a - lum - bran nues - tras al - mas y
Our souls and our minds light up with

nues - tras men - tes._____
hope e - ter - nal._____

Somos los indios rojos puro Atahualpa,
que en nuestra atrición somos como Sigalpa.
Todos dicen que el indio llora en sus quenas,
porque canta con alma sus crueles penas.

We are the redskinned Indians of Atahualpa,
And in our sadness we are just like Sigalpa.
Everyone says the Indian's music's crying;
He sings his heartfelt songs - he can't stop his sighing.

Llanto Del Indio
Lament Of The Indian

Guitar Solo

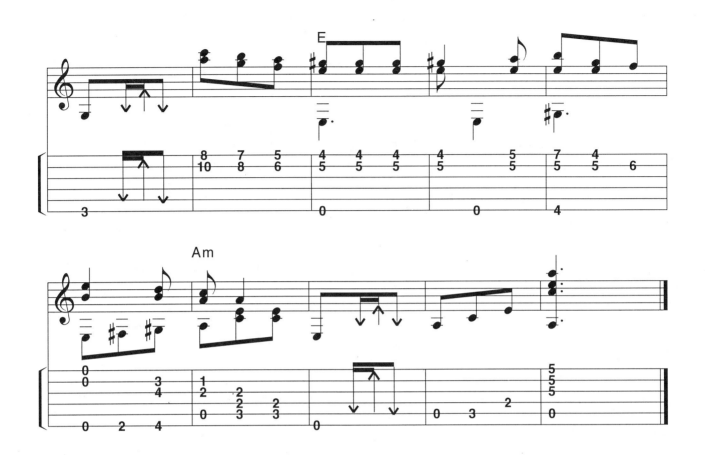

Muchacha Bonita
Pretty Girl

Perú - Song and Accompaniment

Huaino

Mas si has dado a alguno tu vida y tu amor,
Vete bien lejos, lejos de mí,
Muchacha bonita del lindo lunar.

But if you have given your life and your love,
Go far away - so far off from me,
You dear pretty girl with the dark beauty spot.

Muchacha Bonita
Pretty Girl

Problema Social
Social Problem

This song was written by a Puerto Rican in New York in the mid-1940s.

Puerto Rico Song and Accompaniment

By Eduardo Reyes

De_un — a_is - li - ta del Ca - ri - be,
From a Car - ib - be - an is - land,

En bus - ca de tra - ba-jo ven - go yo. A -
Look - ing for a job I ar-rived in town. But

som - bra-do me que - dé con lo que en-con-tré A -
what was my big sur - prise! I can't be - lieve my eyes! Sur -

quí_en los "No - va yor - es" ¿Qu'es e - so? ¡Ju - ro que no sé!
round - ed by New York- ers, What's go - ing on, I can't sur - mise!

Chorus

E

¡Mi - ra———— que soy pro - ble-ma!————
Just look,————— I'm a *pro - ble-ma!*—————

B7   E

¡Ay mi com - pa'e pe - ro que di - le - ma!————
Oh, my dear friend, And what a di - lem - ma!————

Me di - cen u - na mi - no - rí - a;————
They say now that I'm a mi - nor-i-ty;————

B7   E   E7

Pro - ble - ma——— en so-cio-lo - gí - a.————
A big pro - blem in so - ci - o-lo-gy.————

115

Quie - ro ____ so - lo ga - nar u - nos ____ bo - los ____ pa' la de-
I want ____ to earn some mon - ey here ____ so that ____ I can sup-

fen - sa ____ del hu - mil - de ho - gar. Yo no ven - go_a pe-
port my ____ hum - ble fam - i - ly. I don't come ask - ing

dir li - mos - na. Lo que quie - ro es só - lo tra - ba - jar.
cha - ri - ty. What I want now is job se - cu - ri - ty.

Yo, que peleaba en la guerra,	I, who soldiered in the army,
Americano al fín, como nací.	An American, as good as anyone.
Aunque sirvo pa' pelear,	The gun I had to tote
Yo no puedo votar	Did not get me the vote
Pa' el presidente de la patria,	For President, and when I look
Y al venir a trabajar. *Chorus*	For a job, I get their goat. *Chorus*

116

Problema Social
Social Problem

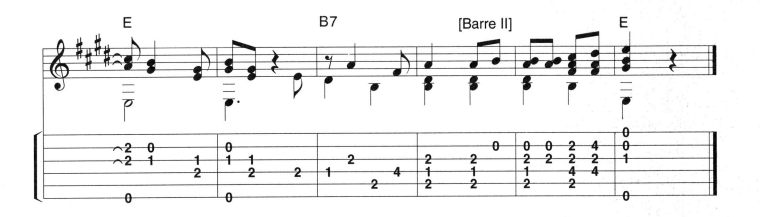

Un Jíbaro En Nueva York
A Peasant In New York

This ten-line verse is called a *décima*. A typical *décima* is frequently improvised by the singer, who may be challenged to create clever, humorous rhymes on the spot.

Puerto Rico - Song and Accompaniment

Me di - jiste_hay co-mo_un mes que tú hablas cual - quier i -
A month a - go you did say, Each and ev-'ry lan - guage you're

dio ma, y_a-ho - ra yo no ha - go broma_y tie - nes que ha-blar in - glés._
knowing, Now's the time that you must be showing, So speak in English to - day._

Ar - ro - dí - lla te_a mis pies sin a - lar - des y sin
Now, kneel down here at my feet, And don't make an - y ex -

rui - dos,_ Y dime_en ver - so me - di - do,_
cu - ses,_ But tell me in meas - ured ver - ses,_

"tur-key." — Y di-cen i-de-a, "i - de-a." Y mie-do, di-cen "a -
"tur-key." — And then for i - de-a, "i - de-a." And mie-do, They say "a -

Last time to Coda 𝄌 𝄌 Coda D6

fri - a," Y_al ra - te-ro, "pick-y pock-ey"
fri - a." And ra - te-ro, "pick-y pock-ey"
[a-fraid]   [pick-pocket]

𝄌 Coda

Woman
Hay alguna analogía
En lo que me has contestado,
Pero aun no has terminado,
Falta mucho todavía.
La vida me apostaría,
Que aunque tomes interés,
Si te diera todo el mes
El chance para pensar,
Tú no podrás hilvanar
Otra décima en inglés.

Man
Al beso le dicen "kiss,"
Para decir la hora dicen "o'clock,"
Y a la señorita, "miss."
Al queso le dicen "cheese,"
Al te amo, "I love you,"
Al orgullo, "ballyhoo."
Le dicen "house" a la casa,
Y para decir "¿Qué pasa?"
todo el mundo dice:
"What's the matter with you?"

Woman
Aunque de todas las redes
Saliste don facultad,
Tengo la seguridad,
Que finalizar no quedes.
Lo van a escuchar ustedes,
Que por su derrota brindo.
Porque sólo cuando eres gringo,
Como aquel guerrero fuerte
Que dijo al pie de la muerte,
"Muero, pero no me rindo."

Man
Y dicen al día, "day,"
Al pobre le dicen "poor."
Al tan bello, "so beautiful,"
Y a lo que está bien, "okey."
Y como cosa de ley,
A la luna dicen '"moon."
Al tono le dicen "tune,"
Y en vez de fín dicen "end."
Venga un aplauso, *my friend,*
Que venga, *very soon.*

Woman
There are some words you do know.
But though you think you are winning,
This is just the very beginning,
You've still a long way to go.
I'd bet my life on it now,
That even if you would wish
To spend another month there,
To rack your brains for a rhyme,
You couldn't make up in time
Another *décima* in English.

Woman
Though you have made no mistakes,
With all the traps I have set you,
I am willing to bet you,
You don't have what it takes,
I celebrate your defeat.
For you will only speak the lingo
When you have become a gringo.
Like that warrior of old,
Who, when facing death, I'm told,
Said "I die, but don't surrender."

Man
They call *beso*"kiss,"
To tell time they say "o'clock,"
And *señorita* they call "miss."
Queso becomes"cheese,"
For *te amo* they say "I love you,"
Orgullo is "ballyhoo."
They say "house" for *casa,*
And for "*¿Qué' pasa?*"
they all say,
"What's the matter with you?"

Man
They call *día* "day,"
For *pobre,* they say "poor."
Tan bello is "so beautiful,"
And what's *bien* is "okay."
And, as the law goes,
Luna is called "moon."
A *tono* is a "tune,"
Instead of *fin* they'll say "end."
Let's hear some applause, my friend,
Let's hear it very soon.

Un Jíbaro En Nueva York
A Peasant In New York

Guitar Solo

La Terrible Inmensidad
The Terrible Immensity

Uruguay Song and Accompaniment

La te-rri-ble_in-men-si - dad_____ en mi des-car-ga sus- pi - ra.
How this im- men - si - ty weighs down It caus-es me to keep sigh - ing,

Los pla - ce - res son men - ti - ra;
Pleas- ures are noth - ing but false- hoods,

Só- lo la pe - na_es ver- dad._____ E - sa tu sed de
On- ly hard-ship is the truth,_____ While for life you are

vi - da,_____ Me tie - ne siem- pre pe-nan-do._____
thirst-ing,_____ It on - ly height-ens the sor-row._____

Con mi destino luchando,	I with my destiny fighting,
Y sin encontrar bonanza,	Never encountering fortune.
Sufriendo está mi esperanza,	Suffering is all I can hope for.
Dime, fortuna, ¿hasta cuándo? *Chorus*	Tell me, o fortune: for how long? *Chorus*

La Terrible Inmensidad
The Terrible Immensity

Sentimientos
Feelings

The *milonga* is a type of folk ballad, known in Uruguay since the middle of the 19th century. Sung by *milongueros,* it may deal with a variety of subjects, from politics and nationalism to *"la conquista de una mujer"* ("the conquest of a woman"). "Sentimientos" is in the ten-line, *décima,* form. The manner of expression in this song is rather convoluted. The repeated first words of each verse—a sort of litany—actually interrupt the flow of thought. The sentence fragments should be judiciously pieced together to make sense out of the tortured soul of the singer. As with its equivalent, the Argentine tango, a *milonga* is invariably a song of sadness and suffering

Uruguay - Song and Accompaniment

Milonga

Di- go que sien- to des - ve - lo,
I say that I'm feel-ing rest-less

Di- go que sien-to_a-flic - ción,
I say that I'm feel-ing grief,

Di- go de co-ra - zón.
I say it from my heart,

Di - go que llo-rar no pue - do;
And I say that I can - not cry;

Di- go que_en mi tris-te sue - lo,
I say that in my sad coun-try,

Di- go que pa-dez-co, sí,
I say I do suf-fer so,

Di-go que pues-to_a su - frir,_____
I say I've been made to suf-fer,

Di-go que den-tro de_un le - cho,
I say that e - ven while rest - ing,

Di-go que den-tro_de mi pe-cho,
I say that deep in my bo-som,

Sien-to_y no sien-to sen - tir._____
I feel with-out hav-ing feel - ings.

Salvo estoy de mi entender,	I am beyond understanding,
Salvo de hacer exigencias,	I am beyond all demands.
Salvo de correspondencia,	I am beyond doing favors,
Salvo me tiene un deber;	I'm beyond all things like that.
Salvo de todo placer,	I am beyond any pleasure,
Salvo estoy porque comprendo,	I am beyond, for I know,
Salvo de una dicha vengo,	I'm beyond, I come from fortune.
Salvo de un buen porvenir,	I am beyond a good future.
Salvo vivo de morir,	I am beyond even dying;
DE UN SENTIMIENTO QUE TENGO.	FROM A FEELING THAT I HAVE.
Quisiera que el más cantor,	I'd like that the finest singer,
Quisiera un consejo darme,	I'd like to get his advice.
Quisiera nunca acordarme,	I'd like never to remember,
Quisiera tener valor;	I'd like never having courage.
Quisiera en este dolor,	I'd like to in all of this pain,
Quisiera hacer dividir,	I'd like to divide it up.
Quisiera para vivir,	I'd like in order to live,
Quisiera el alma serena,	I'd like my soul to be peaceful.
Quisiera apartar las penas,	I'd like to put aside suffering,
QUE HE SENTIDO SIN SENTIR.	THAT I HAVE FELT WITHOUT FEELING.
Tengo en el sentido valor,	I have a feeling of courage,
Tengo cambiado el pesar,	I have changed all of my sorrow.
Tengo que recuperar,	I have to find once again,
Tengo la esperanza en Dios;	I have my faith in the Lord God.
Tengo en este gran dolor,	I have in this mighty aching,
Tengo el alma batiendo,	I have my soul in torment.
Tengo que vivir sufriendo,	I have to live in suffering,
Tengo una pequeña duda,	I have a small doubting question,
Tengo en mi mente segura,	I have in my mind for sure,
QUE ESTOY SIN SENTIR SINTIENDO.	THAT I AM FEELING NO FEELING

Sentimientos
Feelings

Guitar Solo

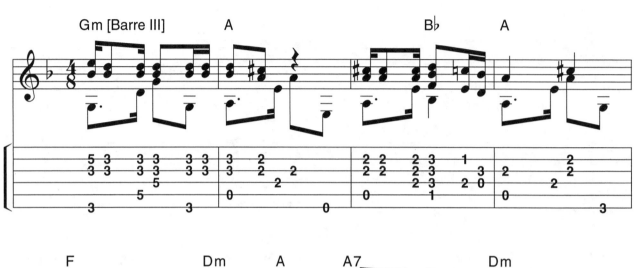

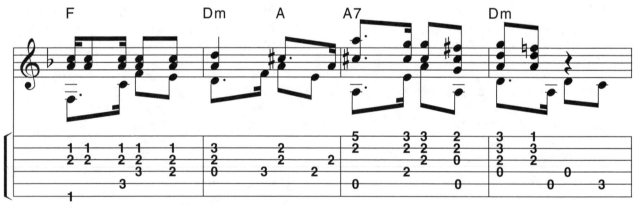

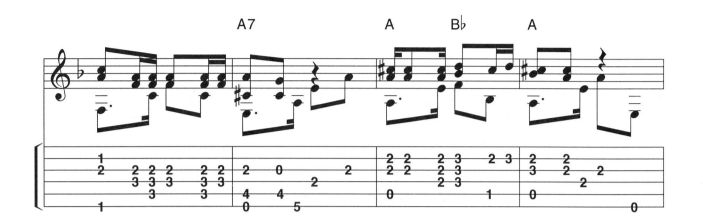

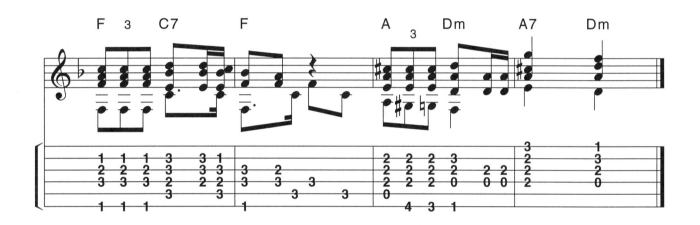

La Mónica Pérez
Monica Perez

A *joropo* is a lively dance.

Venezuela Song and Accompaniment   Joropo

Se-ño-ra Mó-ni-ca Pé - rez, a mi me pa - re - ce bien,
Se-ño-ra Mó-ni-ca Pé - rez, it sure does ap-pear to me,

Que em pa -te-mos los a - mo - res, Si es que lo con sien-te us té
That we should cut short our love, If that is what you real - ly want.

Se ño-ra Mó-ni-ca Pé - rez, mi pa-dri - no me en - se - ñó
Se-ño-ra Mó-ni-ca Pé - rez, My grand-fa - ther, he taught me

a to- mar lo que qui - sie - ra y a us - té me la to - mo yo.
to take what I want and as for me, I think I will take you.

132

La Mónica Pérez
Monica Perez

Guitar Solo

El Carite
The Kingfish

Venezuela Song and Accompaniment

A- yer sa - lió   la lan- cha *Nueva_Es- par- ta.*   Sa- lió con -
The *Nueva_Es-par* - *ta*   set sail yes- ter - day.___   Set out so

fia - da   a   re - co- rrer los   ma- res.   En-con- tró_un pez   de
brave-ly   to   sail a- cross the   o- cean.   It met   a   fish   that

fuer- zas muy li - ge- ro,   Que_a- ga- rra los an - zue- los   y re- vien- ta los gua-
was so ver- y trick- y,   It grap pled with our fish hooks   and it tore up up our

ra- les,   Co- mo la cos- ta_es bo - ni- ta, Yo me ven - go di- vir-
net- ting.   O,   the coast- line is   so   pret- ty, As I sailed   a- long for

tien-do; Pe-ro me vie-ne si-guien-do de fue-ra_u-na pi-ra-güi-ta.
pleas-ure; But I saw ap-proach-ing swift-ly a ca-noe off in the dis-tance.

Ayer salimos muy temprano a pescar	We sailed out early yesterday to fish,
Nos fuimos juntos todos los pescadores	And we were joined by all the fishermen.
Y entre las olas lo vimos saltando	Among the waves we saw how it did leap,
Que iba persiguiendo a los voladores. *Chorus*	As it did chase the silver flying fish. *Chorus*
Un marinero al verlo se alegró	And when a sailor spied him, he was glad
A este sabroso pescado de los mares	To see this tasty fish of the deep ocean.
Y en seguida les dijo a los muchachos	So he then called out loudly to his shipmates,
Preparen los arpones y tiren los guarales. *Chorus*	"Prepare the harpoons, heave away so lively!" *Chorus*
En los ramales del coco lo pescamos	With our long lines of fiber we did fish it,
En lo profundo del mar donde vivía	Down to the depths where he lived in the ocean.
Y lo pescamos en la lancha *Nueva Esparta.*	And we did catch him in the launch *Nueva Esparta,*
Para presentarlo hoy con alegria. *Chorus*	To show it off today with great emotion. *Chorus*
Señores, todos les damos las gracias	Good people, we so gratefully do thank you
Los pescadores se van a marchar.	And now the fishermen are ready to move on.
Nos despedimos con este carite	We take our leave with our great *carite*,
Que les presentamos en este lugar. *Chorus*	Which we have shown you here in our town. *Chorus*

El Carite
The Kingfish

Guitar Solo

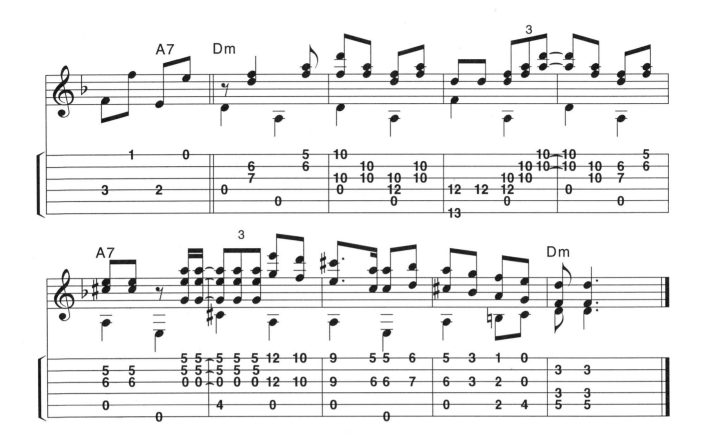